A Bear Cub Grows

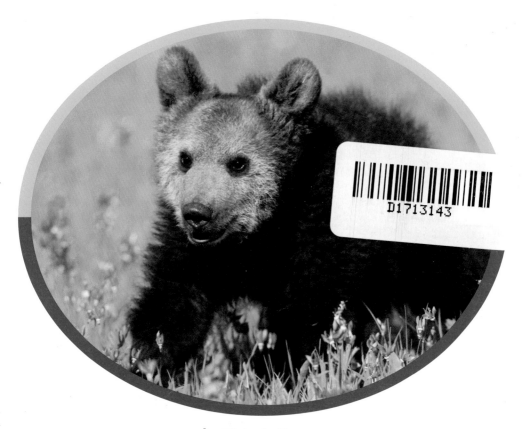

by Victoria Torres

I need to know these words.

bear cub

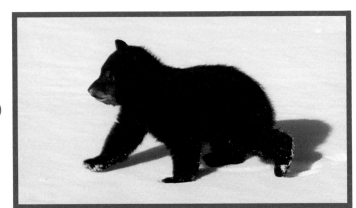

grow

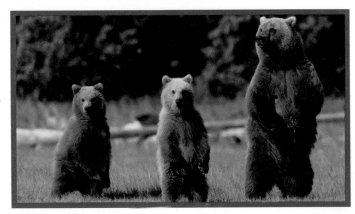

2

sleep

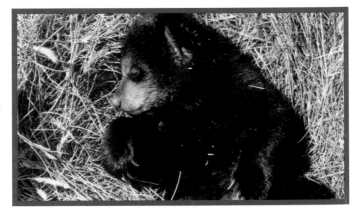

swim

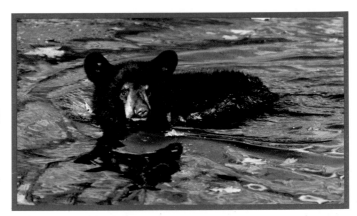

A bear cub can sleep.

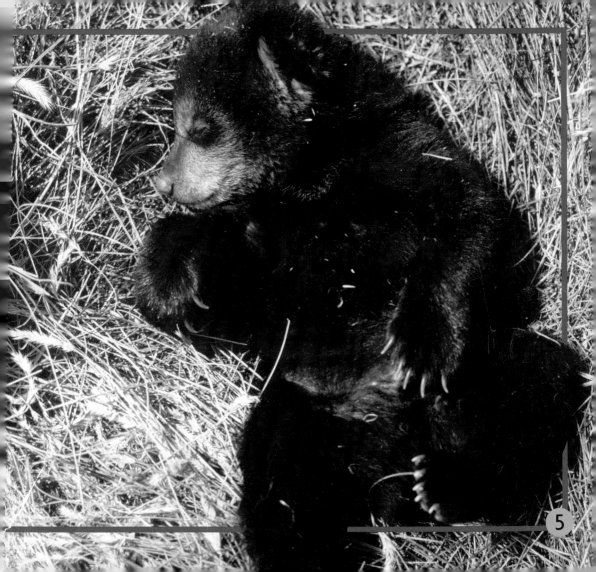

A bear cub can walk.

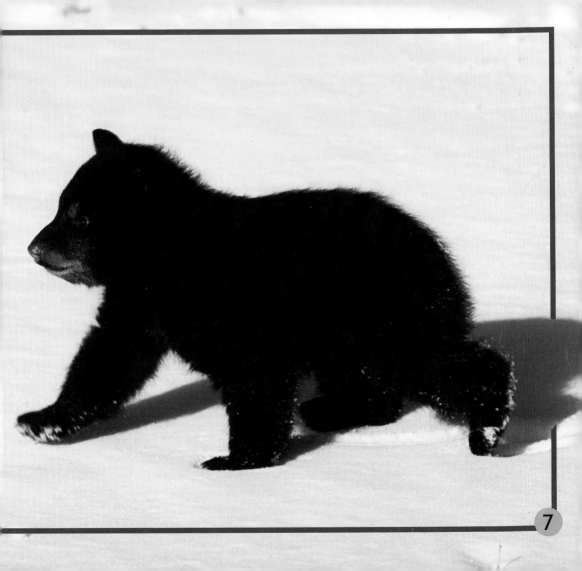

A bear cub can play.

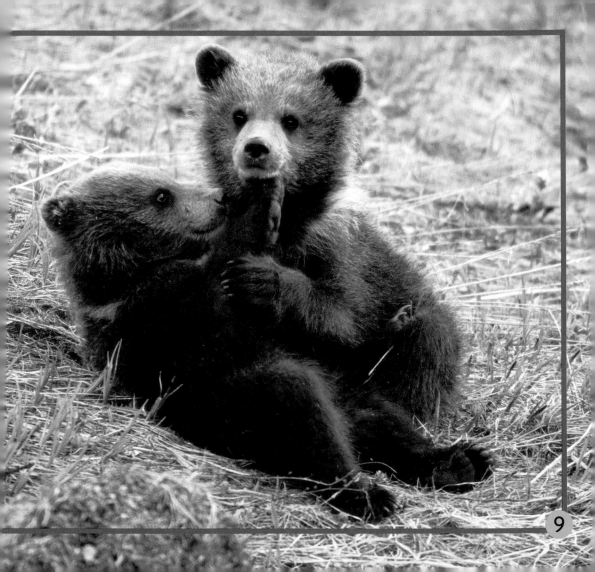

A bear cub can eat.

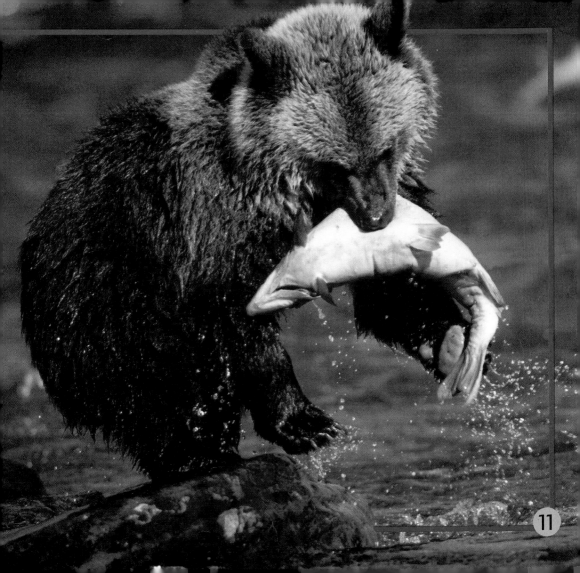

A bear cub can swim.

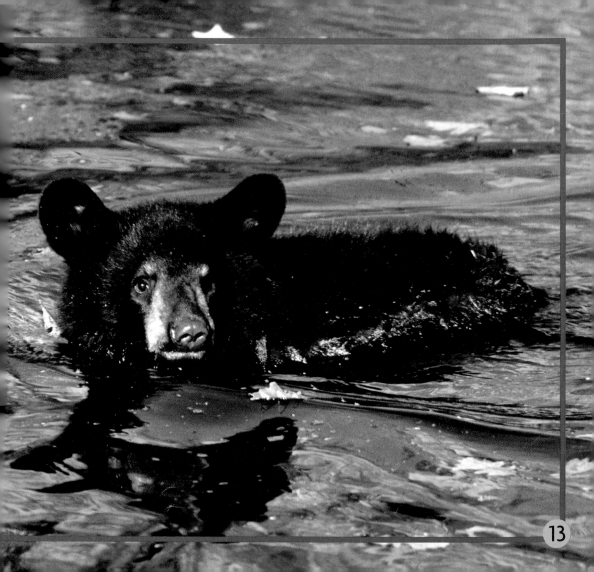

A bear cub can run.

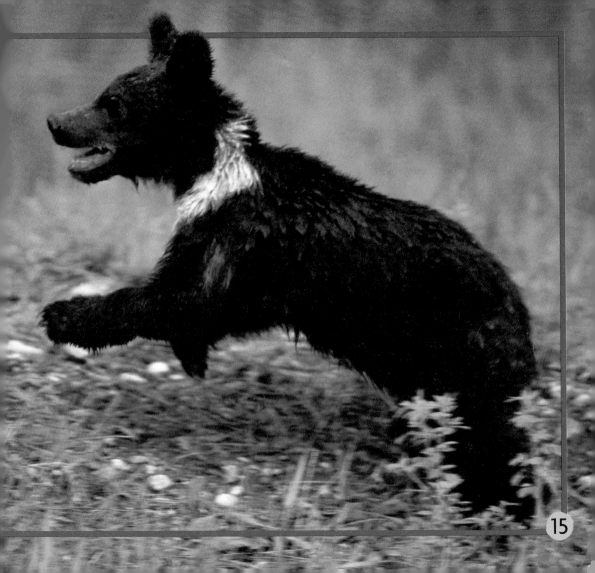

A bear cub can grow.

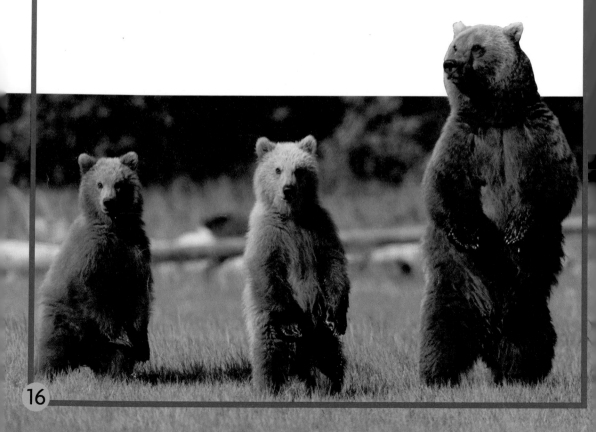